MY FIRST
PAINT

B·O·O·K

DAWN SIRETT

DK

DORLING KINDERSLEY
London • New York • Stuttgart

DK

A Dorling Kindersley Book

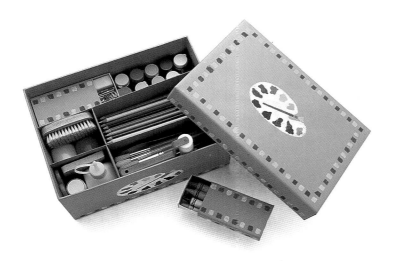

Designer *Mandy Earey*
Photography *Dave King*
Production *Ruth Cobb*

Managing Editor *Jane Yorke*
Managing Art Editor *Chris Scollen*

First published in Great Britain in 1994
by Dorling Kindersley Limited,
9 Henrietta Street, London WC2E 8PS

**A CIP catalogue record for this book is
available from the British Library.**

ISBN 0-7513-5124-5

Colour reproduction by Colourscan, Singapore
Printed and bound in Italy by L.E.G.O.

Dorling Kindersley would like to thank the following for
their help in producing this book: Jane Bull for making
the projects on pages 26, 36, and 39, Mark Richards
for jacket design, Jonathan Buckley, and Rosemary Sirett.
Dorling Kindersley would also like to give special
thanks to the following for appearing in this book:
Victoria Chandler, Josey Edwards, Jade McNamara,
Keat Ng, and Tebedge Ricketts.

Illustrations by Brian Delf

CONTENTS

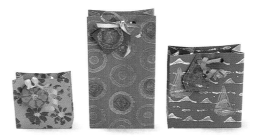

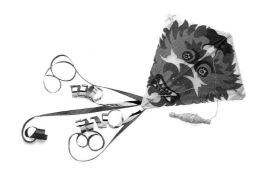

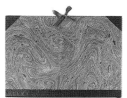

PAINTING BY PICTURES

My First Paint Book shows you how to make and paint all sorts of wonderful things using everyday materials. Step-by-step photographs and simple instructions tell you exactly what to do, and there are life-size photographs of all the finished projects. On the opposite page is a list of things to remember when using this book, and below are the points to look for on each page when making and painting the projects.

How to use this book

What the project is about
The introduction to each project tells you important information about the activity shown.

Equipment
Illustrated checklists show you which tools you will need to have ready before you start each project.

The things you need
The things to collect for each project are shown life-size to help you check that you have everything you will need.

PERFECT PRINTS

Printing is a fun way to use paint and the results look great; thick, sticky paint works best. All sorts of things such as card, vegetables, or even your fingers can be used as printing tools. A sponge on an old baking tray makes a good printing pad. To avoid mixing colours, use one tool for each colour and let the first colour dry when printing one colour over another. Try decorating writing paper and envelopes. You can also print on invitations, greeting cards, or postcards.

EQUIPMENT

Sharp knife

Scissors

Baking tray

Household sponges

Jar of water

You will need

Writing paper

Poster paints

Paintbrush

Printing tools

Small matchbox

Large and small carrots

Button

Cotton bud

Envelopes

A piece of thin household sponge

Plastic drinking straw

Thick card

Corrugated card

Large and small cardboard tubes

Printing the paper

1 Put some damp sponges on an old baking tray. Pour paint and a little water on to the sponges. Spread out the paint with a brush.

2 Ask an adult to cut the carrots. Cut a sponge shape. Press each tool into the paint and place firmly on the paper to make a print**.

3 Print with different colours and tools to make a pattern or picture on the paper. Put more paint on each tool every few prints.

*The paint needs to be thick and sticky.
**Practise on scrap paper first.

The finished prints
Try printing a border, a stamp mark, or a picture on the paper and envelopes. Make sure you leave space to write in!

Tree prints made with sponge and the edge of thick card

Ground printed with the edge of corrugated card

Circle print made with a cardboard tube

Pattern printed with a button and a small tube

Border printed with a triangular piece of sponge

Circle prints made with a cotton bud and a straw

Tractor printed with carrots, a matchbox, the edge of thick card, and a cotton bud

Things to remember

1 Read through all the instructions before you begin a project and gather together everything you will need.

2 Put on an apron or an old shirt before you start and roll up your sleeves.

3 Lay down lots of newspaper to protect work-tables and the floor.

4 Be very careful when using scissors or sharp knives. **Do not use them unless an adult is there to help you.**

5 Always open the windows when using oil-based varnish and ask an adult to clean the brush in white spirit for you.

6 Put everything away when you have finished and clean up any mess.

Step-by-step
Step-by-step photographs and clear instructions tell you exactly what to do at each stage of a project.

Painting tips
Look out for useful tips, which give you extra information about a painting technique.

The finished project
Life-size photographs show you what the finished projects look like, helping you to make them.

PAINTED BOTTLES

Try turning empty bottles or jars into pretty vases and pots. Clean and dry the bottles or jars before you paint them. You can paint glass or plastic, but be very careful with glass: keep the bottle or jar on a table while you paint it. Finish with a coat of varnish so that the paint doesn't rub off.

EQUIPMENT

Jar of water   Saucer

You will need

Medium paintbrush

Thin paintbrush

Poster paints

Empty bottles or jars (plastic or glass)

Clear varnish

PVA glue

Painting the bottle

1 Make sure the bottle or jar is clean and dry. Mix a little PVA glue with the paint. This helps the paint stick to the glass or plastic.

2 Paint a design on the bottle or jar. A simple idea is to dab on dots of paint all over the bottle. Try using lots of different colours.

3 When the paint is dry, paint clear varnish on the bottle or jar. This will protect the paint and give a shiny finish.

PAINTING TIPS
• Keep the paint fairly thick so that it doesn't run.
• If you make a mistake, wipe the paint off before it dries and start again.

The finished bottles and jars

The finished jars and bottles make perfect vases, pencil pots, or brush pots, and are excellent gifts for friends and family.

A border around the rim adds the finishing touch.

Here, one colour has been painted into another.

You can cover the container completely, or leave some glass or plastic showing.

A simple pattern of zigzags, dots, and circles suits this narrow jar.

18

19

5

PAINTING KIT

Here, you can see the tools and equipment that you will need to paint the projects in this book. For most of the activities you can use poster paints, but for some you will need special paints, such as fabric or marbling paints, which you can buy in art and craft shops. Some of the projects are painted with sponges or nailbrushes instead of paintbrushes, and in other projects, pictures or patterns are scratched into paint with plastic knives or forks.

Rags are very useful for cleaning your paintbrushes and other equipment and you will need lots of newspaper to keep your work area clean.

Fabric paints

Marbling paints

Poster paints

Newspaper

Acrylic paints usually come in tubes like this.

Clear varnish protects paint and gives a glossy finish.

Acrylic paints

Even if you only have a few paints, you can make more colours by mixing them together.

Old saucers make good painting palettes.

Ready-mixed, water-based paints

Ready-mixed, water-based paints often come in large squeezy bottles like this one.

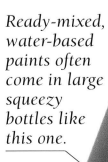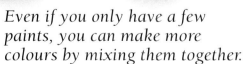

Thick paintbrush

Medium paintbrush

Thin paintbrush

Choose thin brushes with pointed ends for painting fine lines.

Flat paintbrush

Rags

Paint large areas with a thick or flat-ended brush.

Stencil brush

Large, flat paintbrush or old pastry brush

Thin household sponges can be used for painting and to make printing pads.

Printing roller (You can buy these from art and craft shops.)

Old nailbrush or scrubbing brush

Plastic knife and fork

Flour for thickening paint

Use an old baking tray and a sponge as a printing pad.

PVA glue for thickening paint and sticking things

Instead of a saucer, you could use an old bun tin as a palette.

7

PERFECT PRINTS

Printing is a fun way to use paint and the results look great. Thick, sticky paint works best. All sorts of things such as card, vegetables, or even your fingers can be used as printing tools. A sponge on an old baking tray makes a good printing pad. To avoid mixing colours, use one tool for each colour and let the first colour dry when printing one colour over another. Try decorating writing paper and envelopes. You can also print on invitations, greeting cards, or postcards.

You will need

Writing paper

Poster paints

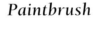

Paintbrush

Printing tools

Large and small carrots

Small matchbox

Button

Envelopes

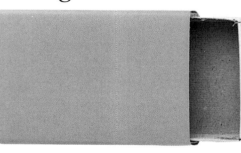

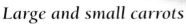

Cotton bud

A piece of thin household sponge

Plastic drinking straw

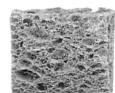

Large and small cardboard tubes

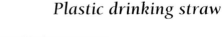

Thick card

Corrugated card

8

Printing the paper

1   Put some damp sponges on an old baking tray. Pour paint and a little water on to the sponges*. Spread out the paint with a brush.

2   Ask an adult to cut the carrots. Cut a sponge shape. Press each tool into the paint and place firmly on the paper to make a print**.

3   Print with different colours and tools to make a pattern or picture on the paper. Put more paint on each tool every few prints.

*The paint needs to be thick and sticky.
**Practise on scrap paper first.

The finished prints

Try printing a border, a stamp mark, or a picture on the paper and envelopes. Make sure you leave space to write in!

Tree prints made with sponge and the edge of thick card

Ground printed with the edge of corrugated card

Circle print made with a cardboard tube

Pattern printed with a button and a small tube

Border printed with a triangular piece of sponge

Circle prints made with a cotton bud and a straw

Tractor printed with carrots, a matchbox, the edge of thick card, and a cotton bud

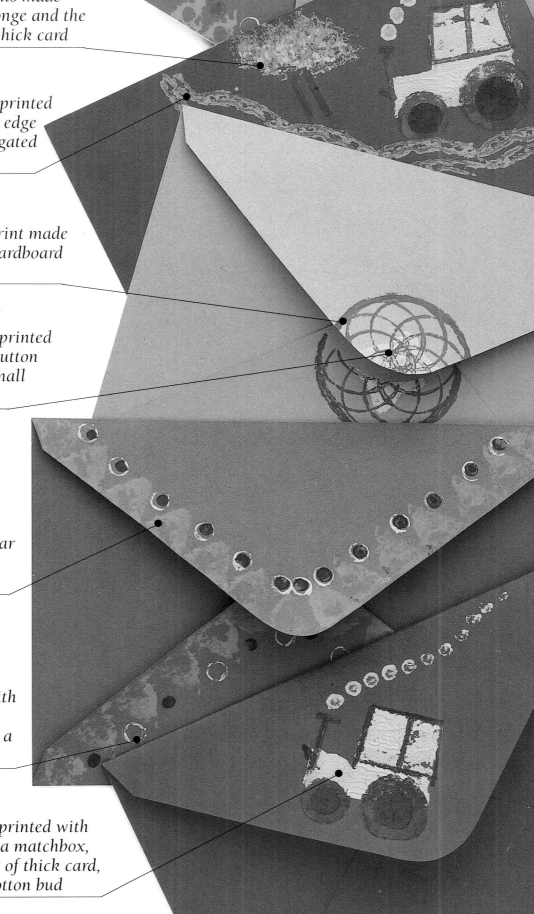

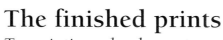

GIFT BAGS

Here, you can find out how to make printing blocks out of modelling clay and create fabulous patterned paper. Use thick paint, sponges, and an old baking tray, as on page 9. You can turn your printed paper into gift bags, or simply use the sheets as wrapping paper. The gift bags are also useful for storing things in.

as on page 9

EQUIPMENT

Pencil   Scissors

Hole punch   Baking tray and household sponges

Ruler   Jar of water

You will need

Gift ribbon

Modelling clay

Paintbrush

Thick paper

Plastic knife

Poster paints

PVA glue

Tracing paper

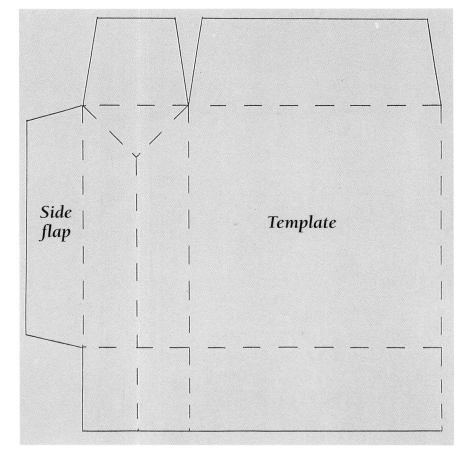

Side flap   *Template*

Making the gift bag

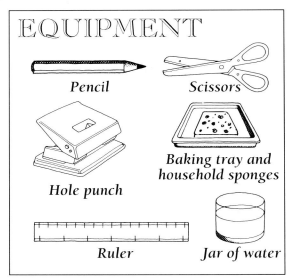

1 Shape a lump of modelling clay. Flatten one side and make marks in it. Use different shaped lumps to make different prints*.

2 Press the clay into the printing pad. Then print a pattern on a sheet of paper. Leave the paint to dry before printing a new colour.

3 Trace the template on to tracing paper with a pencil. Then colour over the lines with the pencil, as shown.

Here, dots are made in a roll of clay and crossed lines are made in a round lump.

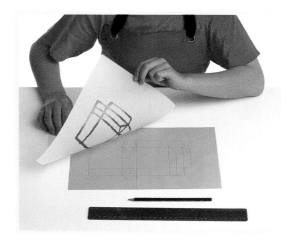

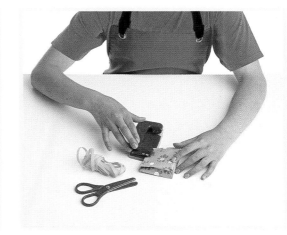

4 Turn over the tracing paper. Place it on the back of the dry printed sheet of paper. Draw over the template twice, as shown**.

5 Cut out the bag pattern. Score along all the lines and fold them, as shown, to make the bag. Glue the side flap and let it dry.

6 Glue the bottom flaps. You can put something heavy in the bag to help them to stick. When dry, punch two holes in the top.

The finished gift bags

Here are some ideas for patterns and colours to print. Gold paint makes an extra special bag. You can make different sized bags by changing the size of the template.

The printing block for the circles was made by pressing a button into a round lump of clay.

Boats and waves

For this block, the outline of a boat was marked into clay and then the whole boat was cut out.

A diamond was marked into a square of clay to make the printing block for the blue diamonds.

For the waves block, the outline of waves was marked into clay and then the clay around the outline was cut away.

GIFT TAGS

Cut out small rectangles of the paper and fold them to make tags. You can then cut the folded rectangles into other shapes, if you wish. Use a hole punch to make a hole for the ribbon.

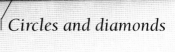

Circles and diamonds

Flowers

**Leave off the side flap the second time you draw over the lines of the template.*

11

WONDERFUL WAX

Wax and paint do not mix, but they can be used together to create an exciting picture. Here, thick paint is painted over wax crayon and then scratched off to make a picture of colourful fireworks. You can scratch out a night-time scene, an animal, a pattern, or anything you like. Find out how to frame your picture on page 46.

how to frame your picture on page 46.

EQUIPMENT

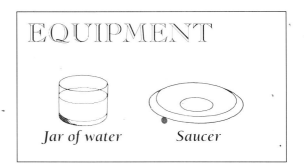

Jar of water　　*Saucer*

You will need

Ice-lolly stick

Wax crayons

Light-coloured paper　　*Black poster paint*

Plastic knife

Thin paintbrush

Thick paintbrush

Making the picture

1 Use brightly coloured wax crayons to draw a pattern on a sheet of paper. Fill the sheet of paper with the pattern.

2 Paint over the pattern with thick black paint. Make sure the pattern is completely covered. You may need two coats of paint.

3 When the paint is dry, draw a picture by scratching off the paint with a plastic knife, a lolly stick, or the end of a paintbrush.

The finished picture

When the black paint is scratched off, you can see the crayon underneath. Bright colours show up well, so use as many brightly coloured crayons as you have to make the pattern.

You can use the ice-lolly stick to scrape off large areas of paint.

The end of a paintbrush makes a medium mark.

You can find out how to scratch shapes into wet paint on page 44. The marks on the frame were made in this way.

Painted card frame

Zigzags, swirls, and stars make brilliant, exploding fireworks!

FRAME IT!

A frame adds the finishing touch to a picture. You can find out how to make picture frames on page 46.

Thin or thick marks can be scratched out with the plastic knife.

13

STENCIL DESIGNS

Stencilling is a fun way to repeat a picture or pattern. A stencil is a piece of card with shapes cut out of it. To stencil, you hold the card flat on a surface and paint through the holes.

You can stencil on walls, furniture, or fabrics, but check with an adult first. Below, a palette and border of squares are stencilled on an art box. You can make up a picture or pattern to stencil. Leave a few centimetres of card around your designs and varnish the stencils to make them hard-wearing.

Practise using your stencils on scrap paper. You will need thick poster paints or acrylic paints and a stencil brush or a sponge to paint with.

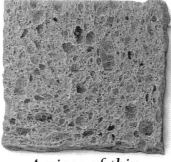

A piece of thin household sponge

EQUIPMENT

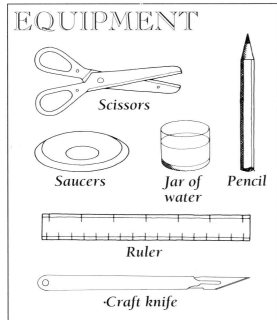

Scissors

Saucers

Jar of water

Pencil

Ruler

·Craft knife

You will need

Clear varnish

Paintbrush for varnishing the stencils

Stencil brush (or a brush with short, stiff hairs)

Poster paints (or you can use acrylic paints)

Making the box

1 Cut two pieces of card to fit the length of the box. Make them twice the depth of the box and fold them in half, as shown.

2 Paint or cover two matchboxes. Cut a length of card to go across the box*. Make it twice the depth and fold it in half, as before.

The card should fit across the box from one side to the matchboxes, as shown.

3 Cut a slit half way down one long partition and another half way up the short partition, so that they slot together, as shown.

14

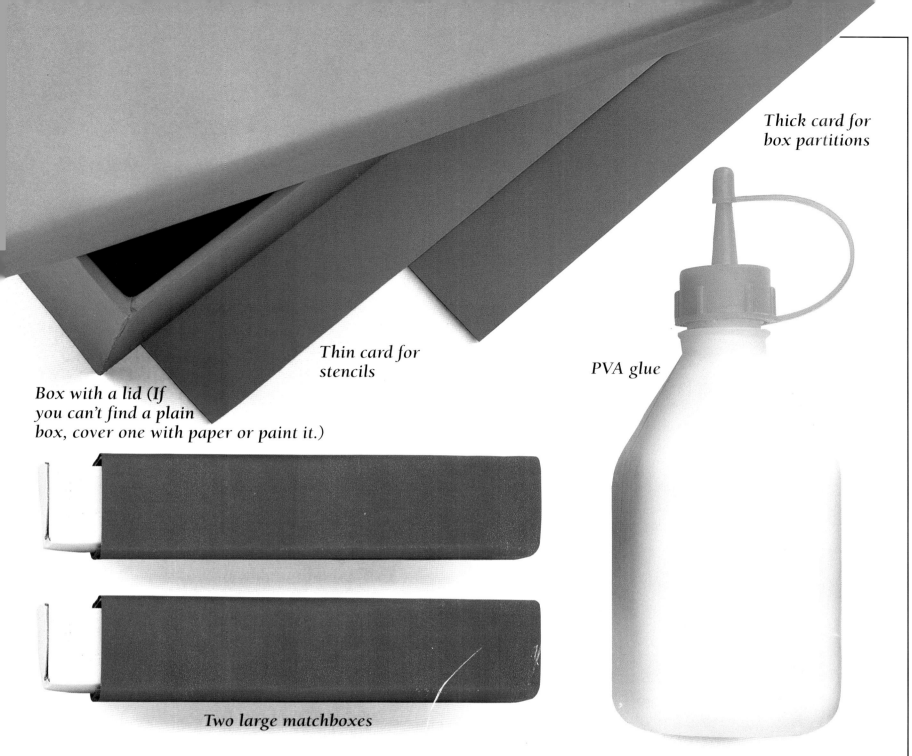

Thick card for box partitions

Thin card for stencils

PVA glue

Box with a lid (If you can't find a plain box, cover one with paper or paint it.)

Two large matchboxes

Stencilling the box

1 Draw a pattern or picture on a piece of card. Ask an adult to cut out your design. Varnish both sides of the card. Leave it to dry.

2 Decide where you want your design to go on the box. Hold the stencil flat**. Paint in the holes with a stencil brush or sponge.

**If you find it hard to hold the stencil in place, tape it down with masking tape.*

3 You can use more than one stencil to make a picture or pattern. Wait for the first colour to dry before stencilling over it.

15

STENCILLED ART BOX

Your stencilled design can be repeated on each side of the art box, and on the lid, and the matchboxes, too. You can fill the box with all kinds of painting and drawing equipment. The bigger compartments can hold paintbrushes, paints, and pencils. The matchboxes are perfect for paper clips, rubbers, or crayons. You might have room for other items, such as your scissors and roller, sponges, modelling tools, modelling clay, and varnish. The box could also be used to store jewellery, sewing equipment, or a collection.

Matchboxes make small compartments. Use as many as you need.

The three partitions divide the box into large and small compartments, which can hold different sized objects.

A PLACE FOR EVERYTHING

Before you cut out your partitions, put everything you want the art box to hold into the box. This will help you to work out the best way to divide up your box.

STENCILLING TIPS

• You may find it easier to paint the outside edge of the stencil hole first and work inwards.
• To avoid smudging the paint, don't take the stencil away until the paint is dry.
• Use thick, sticky paint so that it doesn't run under the stencil.

The line of small red and yellow squares makes a decorative border.

Simple shapes work well when stencilled, such as these squares.

Colourful artist's palette design

PAINTING THEME
Two stencils were used for the palette design. First, the palette was stencilled in white and left to dry. Then the second stencil was held over the palette and the blobs of paint and brush were stencilled on top.

White palette stencilled first

Paints and brush stencilled over palette

Border of squares

17

PAINTED BOTTLES

Try turning empty bottles or jars into pretty vases and pots. Clean and dry the bottles or jars before you paint them. You can paint glass or plastic, but be very careful with glass: keep the bottle or jar on a table while you paint it. Finish with a coat of varnish so that the paint doesn't rub off.

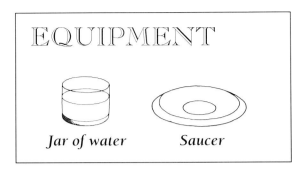
You will need

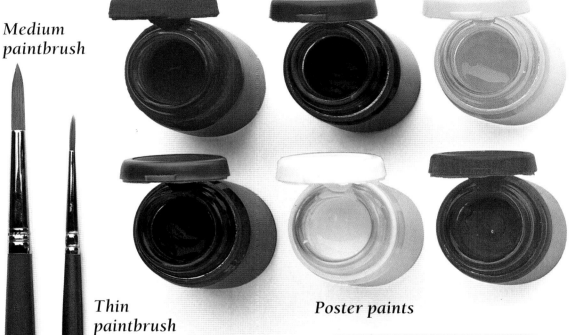

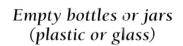
Medium paintbrush

Thin paintbrush

Poster paints

Empty bottles or jars (plastic or glass)

Clear varnish

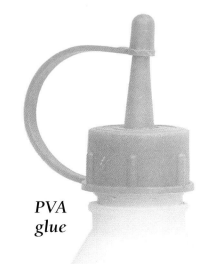

PVA glue

Painting the bottle

1 Make sure the bottle or jar is clean and dry. Mix a little PVA glue with the paint. This helps the paint stick to the glass or plastic.

2 Paint a design on the bottle or jar. A simple idea is to dab on dots of paint all over the bottle. Try using lots of different colours.

3 When the paint is dry, paint clear varnish on the bottle or jar. This will protect the paint and give a shiny finish.

18

The finished bottles and jars

The finished jars and bottles make perfect vases, pencil pots, or brush pots, and are excellent gifts for friends and family.

A border around the rim adds the finishing touch.

Here, one colour has been painted into another.

PAINTING TIPS

• Keep the paint fairly thick so that it doesn't run.
• If you make a mistake, wipe the paint off before it dries and start again.

You can cover the container completely, or leave some glass or plastic showing.

A simple pattern of zigzags, dots, and circles suits this narrow jar.

T-SHIRT PAINTING

Paint your own T-shirts and then wear your original designs! You will be amazed at how easy it is to make them. You can create a unique pattern every time by splattering one colour or more on to the fabric. Always remember to lay down lots of newspaper when flicking paint in this way.

You will need special fabric paints for this project. These can be bought from art and craft shops. Check the instructions that come with your paints. You may need to ask an adult to iron your T-shirt on the reverse side to fix the paint when it has dried.

Turn the page to see the finished splattered T-shirt. You will also find some other ideas for painting on fabric.

Turn the page to see the finished splattered T-shirt.

EQUIPMENT

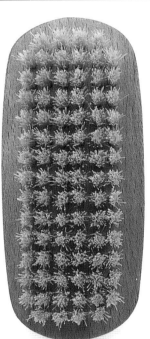

Jar of water   Scissors

Ruler

Pencil

Craft knife

You will need

Masking tape

Fabric paints (Choose colours that will show up well on your T-shirt.)

Old nailbrush or scrubbing brush

T-shirt

Splattering the T-shirt

Plastic knife

Large, flat brush for flicking paint

Two sheets of corrugated card (slightly larger than the T-shirt)

Paintbrush

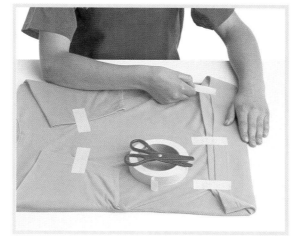

1 Push one sheet of card into the shirt to stop the paint soaking through*. Tape the sleeves and bottom of the shirt, as shown.

2 Draw a square with 20 cm sides in the middle of the other sheet of card. Ask an adult to cut out the square, leaving a frame.

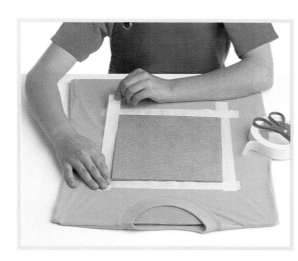

3 Place the cut-out square in the middle of the front of the shirt. Mark the position of the square with tape. Then remove the square.

4 Line up the frame with the tape on the T-shirt and tape it down, as shown. Cover any parts of the T-shirt that still show.

5 Put fabric paint on a nailbrush. Use a plastic knife to flick the paint away from your body and on to the shirt. Leave the paint to dry.

6 Dip a large brush into a new colour. Splatter the paint on to the T-shirt. When dry, ask an adult to iron the shirt to fix the paint**.

*Cut the card to fit inside the T-shirt.

**First check the instructions that come with your paints.

21

DAZZLING DESIGNS

Here are three finished T-shirts plus some ideas for other things that you can decorate with fabric paints. Try painting a pair of socks or a baseball cap to match your T-shirt, or use your paints to brighten up old handkerchiefs, pillow-cases, tablecloths, or cotton scarves.

As well as splattering on fabric, you can print, stencil, or simply paint a picture with a brush. Turn to pages 8, 10, 14, and 28 for instructions on printing and stencilling.

Printed daisy

SOCKS TO MATCH
Try painting a pair of socks to match your T-shirt.

FABRIC PAINTING TIPS

• Ask an adult to iron the fabric first so that it is completely flat when you paint it.
• Always put a thick sheet of card under the fabric because the paint will soak through.
• The fabric will absorb a lot of paint so you may need two coats. Leave the first coat to dry before you paint the second.

SPLATTER PATTERN

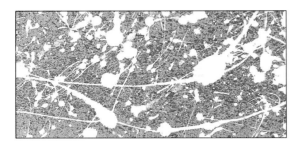

PRINTED DAISIES

STENCILLED CAR

Above are the T-shirt designs close-up.

SPLATTERED SQUARE

A little fabric paint goes a long way when splattering. Load your brush with paint and keep splattering and flicking until no more paint comes off.
You can also make a splatter picture on paper. Turn to page 47 to see a framed splatter picture.

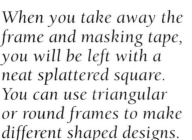

When you take away the frame and masking tape, you will be left with a neat splattered square. You can use triangular or round frames to make different shaped designs.

You can splatter the back of the shirt as well as the front.

Printed spots

Stencilled car

SPOTTY HANDKERCHIEF
Turn a plain cotton handkerchief into a spotty one. A cotton bud was used to print these spots.

CAP
Try stencilling a design on the peak of a cap.

VEHICLE STENCILS
Three stencils have been used on this shirt. The white rectangles were sponged on first. Then the blue car and truck were stencilled on top. Turn to page 14 for instructions on stencilling.

DAISY PRINTS
Modelling clay was used to make the printing blocks for the daisies on this shirt (see page 10 for this technique). Chains of daisies have been printed across the front and back of the T-shirt and around the sleeves.

You can touch up any faint prints with a paintbrush.

PAINTED PEBBLES

Turn pebbles into colourful painted fish and create an amazing underwater world for them to swim in! The pebbles hang in a shallow box on invisible thread. Look on the beach or in a park for different-sized pebbles or stones and fish-like shapes. Find some pictures of tropical fish to give you ideas on how to paint them. Turn the page to see the finished seascape.

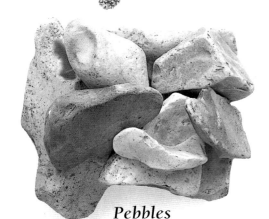

Seaside collection

EQUIPMENT

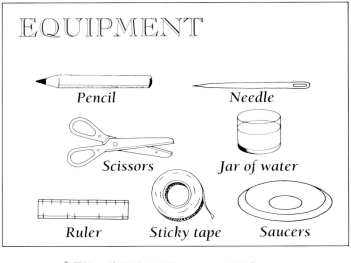

Pencil

Needle

Scissors

Jar of water

Ruler

Sticky tape

Saucers

You will need

Clear varnish

Pebbles

A piece of thin household sponge

Poster paints

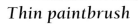

Medium paintbrush

Thin paintbrush

Large, shallow cardboard box

Card

Paper

PVA glue

Invisible thread or clear fishing line

Making the seascape

1 Paint or glue paper over any writing on your box to give it a neat finish. You may need two coats of paint if you paint the box.

2 Paint a sandy seabed and an underwater background on the inside of the box. Try dabbing on paint with a sponge.

3 Draw sea plants and corals on card and cut them out. Fold over the bottom of the plants and corals so that they stand up.

4 Paint the plants and corals with a sponge. When dry, glue along the flaps and stick them to the bottom of the box to make a scene.

5 Wash and dry the pebbles. Mix some white paint with PVA glue and use this to paint an undercoat on the pebbles. Leave them to dry.

6 Put the pebbles on a saucer so you can turn them without touching them. Use paints mixed with PVA glue to paint the pebbles.

7 When the paint is dry, varnish the pebbles to protect the paint. When they are dry, tie a length of thread around each pebble*.

8 Ask an adult to use a needle to pull the lengths of thread through the top of the box, as shown**. Tape down the ends.

9 Arrange shells, driftwood, or stones in the base of the box. You can paint sea animals on more pebbles and add these as well.

*We have used black thread to show you what to do. You should use invisible thread.
**Hold the fish in place first to work out how many threads you need and where you want them to hang.

25

FISHY SCENE

You can keep the finished underwater scene on a table, bookshelf, or window-sill. Use as many fish and shells as you like. If you tap the box gently, all the fish will move, just as if they are swimming in the water!

SETTING THE SCENE

Wait for everything to dry before you assemble the scene. Hang the fish at different levels so that they fill the box.

PLANTS AND CORALS

You can add depth to the scene by positioning large sea plants and corals at the back and smaller ones in the middle and at the front of the box. The fish can swim in between the plants and corals.

SHOALS OF FISH

Fish often swim together in groups or "shoals". Here the orange, yellow, and blue fish have been arranged into groups.

As well as fish, you can paint sea plants, crabs, or other sea creatures on stones.

Make a seaside collection of shells, stones, small rocks, or drift-wood for the seabed.

You can leave some of the box showing to add texture to the scene.

The outside of the box has been covered with blue paper.

If the thread slips off the pebbles, use clear tape to hold it in place.

MIXING COLOURS

Different shades of blue have been made for the background by mixing up different amounts of blue and white paint. The paint has been dabbed on with a sponge.

FABULOUS FISH!

The pebbles were painted in two stages. The base colour was painted first. Once dry, eyes, fins, and scales were painted on top with a thin brush.

The plants and corals were painted by dabbing on orange, green, and white paint with a sponge. Try sponging one colour over another.

27

ANIMAL FRIEZE

Here, you can find out how to make printing blocks by gluing string on to thick card. You can use the blocks to print a frieze to go round the walls of your room. Try making a printing block of your favourite animal. Keep the string picture simple – just an outline is best.

EQUIPMENT

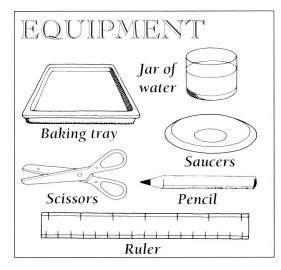

Jar of water

Baking tray

Saucers

Scissors

Pencil

Ruler

You will need

Thick coloured paper

Thick card

Thin string

A piece of thin household sponge

PVA glue

Cotton bud

Paintbrush

Leaves

Printing roller or a wide decorating brush

Ready-mixed, water-based paints*

28

You can buy these in large squeezy bottles (see page 6).

Making the blocks

1 Draw the outline of an animal on a piece of thick card. You can draw any animal or trace the elephants on the next page.

2 Glue lengths of string to the outline. Use shorter lengths of string for eyes and ears. When the glue is dry, cut around the animal.

3 To finish the printing block, glue the string animal to another piece of thick card, as shown. Leave it to dry.

Printing the frieze

1 Put some paint in an old baking tray. Paint the string printing block with a printing roller or a wide decorating brush.

2 Place the block face down on a long strip of thick paper. Press down firmly on the back of the block. Then lift it up carefully.

3 Print enough animals to fill the paper. You can print a background with leaves, a sponge, a piece of card, and a cotton bud.

The finished frieze

In this frieze, the trunks and tails of elephants link up to make a chain!

Red and green paints were mixed together to make brown.

Try painting the back of leaves with a brush and then printing them on to the paper.

You can use a larger or smaller animal to start and finish the frieze.

Tusks painted with a cotton bud

Grass printed with the edge of card

Branches painted with a cotton bud

Ground printed with sponge

STRING PRINTING TIPS

• Practise on scrap paper first.
• It may take a couple of coats of paint to make your string block print because the string will soak up a lot of paint.
• If there are gaps in some of your prints, fill them in with a paintbrush.

ELEPHANTS ON THE MARCH

You can make the frieze as long or as short as you want.

A Diamond Kite

Make, paint, and fly a colourful kite with a wonderful dragon-face design! The kite is made from a large plastic bag. Look for a bag without any writing on it, such as a large bin liner. Acrylic paints work best on plastic. If you don't have these, you can mix a little PVA glue with poster paint, but you may find that some of the paint peels off the plastic.

Plant canes are used for the kite spars. They make a frame for the plastic. Medium-sized canes (46 cm long) should be the correct size. If they are too long, ask an adult to trim them.

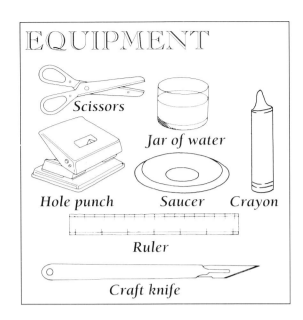

Equipment

Scissors

Jar of water

Hole punch   Saucer   Crayon

Ruler

Craft knife

You will need

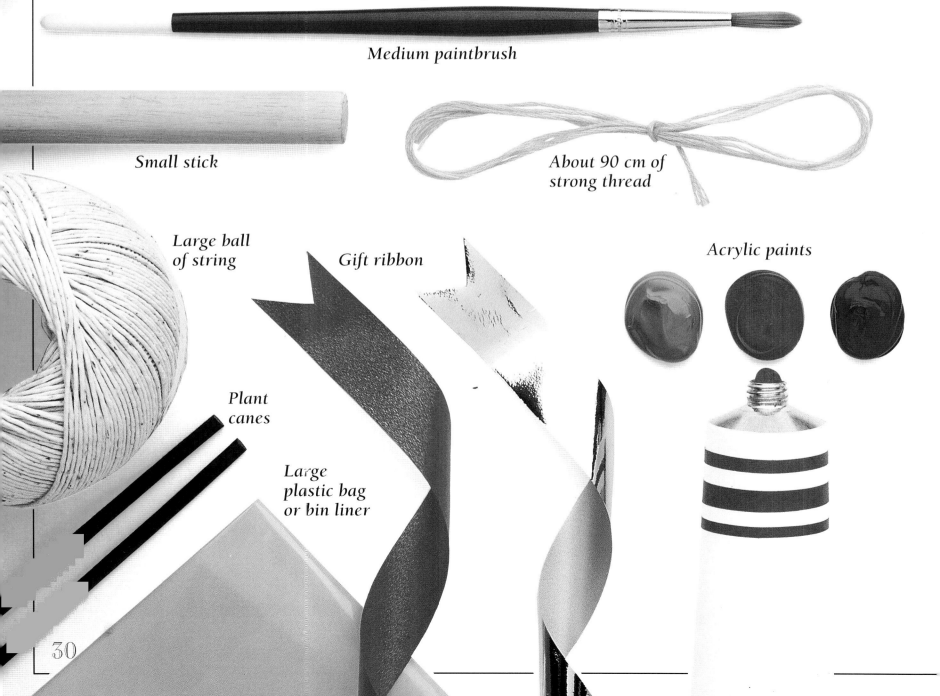

Strong sticky tape

Thin paintbrush

Medium paintbrush

Small stick

About 90 cm of strong thread

Large ball of string

Gift ribbon

Acrylic paints

Plant canes

Large plastic bag or bin liner

Making the kite

1 Cut out a 48 cm square from a plastic bag. Make three marks 14 cm down from the top, and three along the centre, as shown*.

2 Join up the marks on the edge of the plastic. Check that the plastic is about 1 cm bigger than the canes all round. Cut out the kite.

3 Stick tape to the front and back of the kite: on the centre line (11 cm from the top, and 7 cm from the bottom) and across the corners.

4 Fold each corner and punch through the folds to make two holes in each corner. Ask an adult to cut two slits on the centre line**.

5 Paint a design on the kite and leave it to dry. Cut long lengths of gift ribbon. Hold them together and punch a hole in one end.

6 Turn over the kite. Thread one cane through the holes across the kite, as shown. Wrap tape over each end to hold the cane in place.

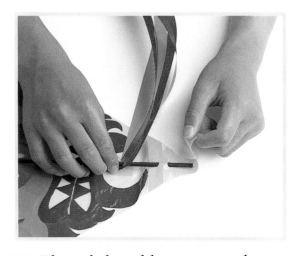

7 Thread the ribbons on to the other cane. Push it into the top and bottom holes, and under the first cane. Tape over the cane ends.

8 Turn over the kite. Push the ends of the thread through the slits in the kite's centre and tie them to the upright cane at the back.

9 Tie a small loop in the thread. It should be at a right angle to the kite, as shown. This is the kite's bridle.

*Fold the plastic in half to find the centre.

**Cut the slits through the tape pieces you placed on the centre line in step 3.

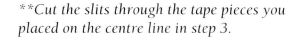

FLYING DRAGON

Attaching the string

1 Wrap tape round each end of a small stick. Tie one end of a large ball of string to the stick and wind on about 30m of the string.

2 When you are ready to fly your kite, tie the end of the string to the loop in the bridle. Knot it two or three times.

LAUNCHING THE KITE

When you want to fly your kite, make sure the string is tied securely to the bridle and stick. Find an open space. Unwind a little string. On a windy day, the kite should fly from your outstretched arm, or you can ask a friend to hold the kite at a distance and let go when it fills with wind. Once your kite is up, slowly let out more string.

Pull on the string and watch your kite rise up into the air!

Stand with your back to the wind and hold the stick at each end.

If your kite doesn't fly very well, try adjusting the angle of the loop in the bridle.

A long tail looks spectacular and keeps your kite steady. Red and gold ribbons suggest fire coming from the dragon's mouth.

The finished kite

You can copy this face or paint a different face on your kite – try an octopus, a lion, or a monster.

DO'S AND DON'TS

• Never fly your kite in strong winds or stormy weather.
• Never fly near overhead cables, roads, cars, buildings, trees, people, animals, or an airport.
• Always wear gloves when kite-flying.
• Never look directly at the Sun and always wear sunglasses to protect your eyes.

The thick tape strengthens the plastic.

*The ends of the thread
are pushed through
the slits and tied to
the upright cane.*

*Make sure that the plant
canes lie on the side of the kite
that isn't painted and that they
hold the plastic fairly taut.*

MAKING A COLLAGE

Everyday things can be used in a collage. Make a collection of materials that you think would look interesting. You don't have to use the materials shown: dried pasta shells, grains of uncooked rice, sand, fabric, string, and magazine cut-outs are just a few more ideas.

Below, a city scene is made with collage materials. Turn the page to see the finished picture and for some ideas for different collages.

EQUIPMENT

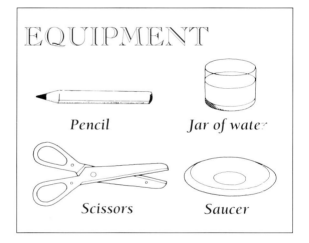

Pencil

Jar of water

Scissors

Saucer

You will need

Small box

PVA glue

Poster paints

Making the collage

1 Cut out and arrange your collage materials on thick card to make a picture. Work out the main parts of your collage first.

2 When you are happy with your picture, glue the materials on to the thick card. Build up layers to make the collage stand out.

3 Different shapes and textures will add variety to your collage. Here, strips of corrugated card are used to make a pattern.

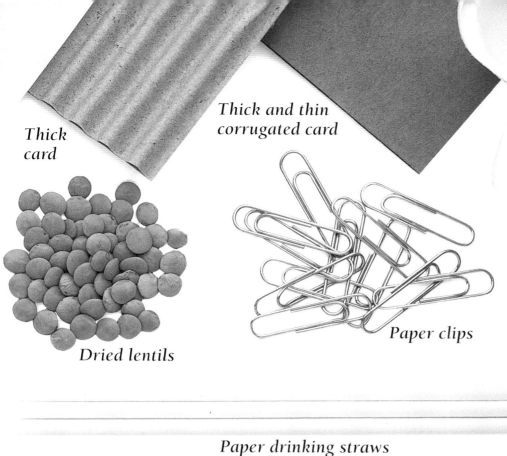

Thick card

Thick and thin corrugated card

Dried lentils

Paper clips

Cardboard egg box

Paper drinking straws

Plastic vegetable pot

Plastic drinking straws

Dried spaghetti

Thin paintbrush

Medium paintbrush

Painting the collage

1 When the glue is dry, paint the collage. Mix each colour with a little PVA glue to help the paint coat the plastic materials*.

2 Paint the background. You can build up texture by adding more PVA glue to the paint to thicken it.

3 Small things, such as paper clips or lentils, can be used to add detail. Stick them into the paint on the collage before it dries.

Mixing the paint with glue also allows you to stick small things straight into the wet paint.

CITY SKYLINE

Here is the finished city scene. Tall buildings have been made with different types of card and parts of a plastic vegetable pot. You can make a collage of anything you like: try a countryside scene, a picture of a farm, or the street where you live.

CARD BACKGROUND
Stick your materials on to thick card. Paper won't be strong enough to hold them.

STICKY PAINT
You can stick small things into the wet paint if it has been mixed with PVA glue.

Paper clips

Smaller buildings are stuck on to the taller buildings. This makes the taller buildings look as if they are in the distance.

Plastic vegetable pot

Plastic straws and strips of corrugated card make a door.

Paper clips, pasta, or pulses can be arranged into interesting patterns.

Paint has been thickened with PVA glue to add texture to the cloudy sky.

Lentils

Dried spaghetti

Plastic
vegetable pot

You can leave some parts
of the collage unpainted.

Thin strips of
corrugated card
have been used
to make a crane.

CHOOSING COLOURS

Think about the colours that you are going to use. Browns, greys, blues, oranges, and yellows have been mixed and used to paint the stone, brick, concrete, and metallic buildings in this city scene.

Part of a cardboard egg box makes a perfect roof for this building.

Paper straws are used to make windows.

A FITTING FRAME!

The collage has been framed with corrugated card. You can learn how to make this frame on page 47.

Thin strips of
corrugated card

Cardboard box

BADGES AND BROOCHES

With some card, papier-mâché, and poster paint, you can design and paint a badge in any shape you like: try making your favourite animal, machine, vehicle, a round face, a sun, or a moon. The finished badges make wonderful gifts for your friends or family.

To make the papier-mâché mixture for the badges, you need to tear newspaper into tiny pieces and then mix the pieces with a little water and wallpaper paste. It should be a very smooth, dough-like mixture. Leave your papier-mâché badges to dry overnight before you start to paint them.

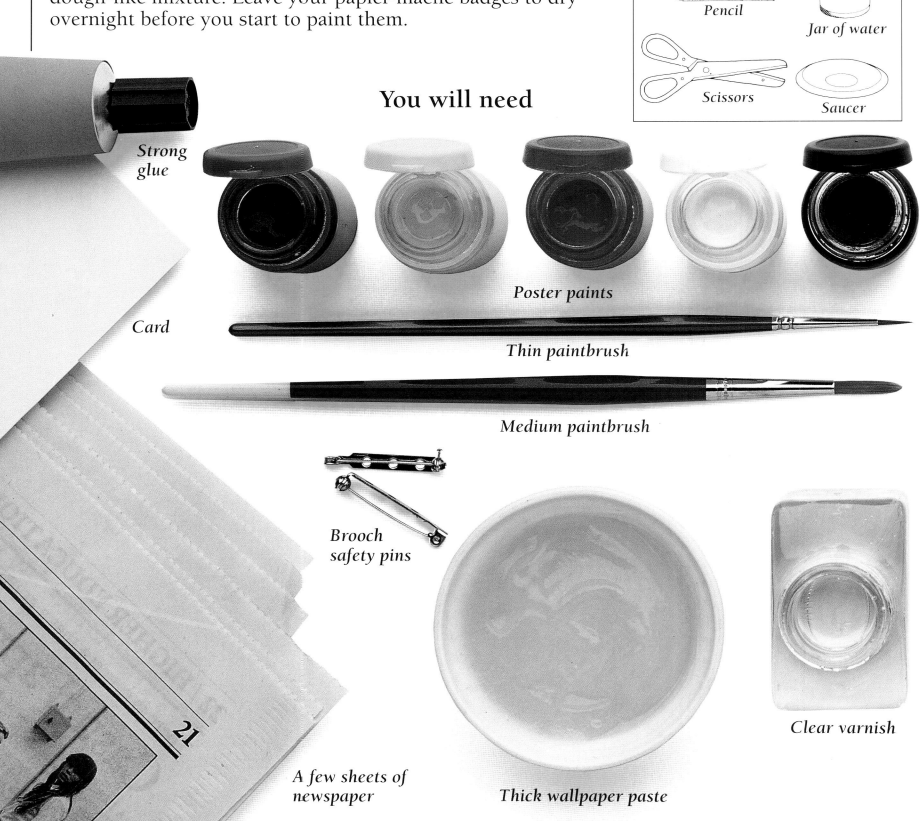

EQUIPMENT

Dish

Spoon

Pencil

Jar of water

Scissors

Saucer

You will need

Strong glue

Card

Poster paints

Thin paintbrush

Medium paintbrush

Brooch safety pins

A few sheets of newspaper

Thick wallpaper paste

Clear varnish

21

Making the badges

1 Draw a shape on card and cut it out. Tear newspaper into tiny pieces and mix with a little water and wallpaper paste in an old dish.

2 Mash up the papier-mâché until it has the texture of dough. Put some on the card. Shape the papier-mâché and leave it to dry overnight.

3 Paint a design on the front and paint the back in one colour. Leave the badge to dry. Glue the pin to the back. Varnish the badge.

The finished badges

A thin paintbrush will help you to paint detail on the small badges. Here are some different designs.

The varnish makes the badges stronger and gives a shiny finish.

BOAT

DINOSAUR

Here, papier-mâché has been shaped to look like fur.

Papier-mâché was built up to make the frame on this badge.

DOG

SUN FACE

FRAMED PICTURE

Leave one colour to dry before you paint the next.

BUTTERFLY

CAR

MARBLING PAPER

Try making beautiful marbled papers and then use them to cover a folder. Marbling paper is great fun. Special paints are dripped into water and form patterns on the surface. You then place paper on the water to pick up the paint. Marbling paints are usually sold as part of a kit. You may need to thicken the water with a special powder before you drip in the paint, so check the kit's instructions. You can also use oil paints. Ask an adult to thin the paints with white spirit and add a little vinegar to the water.

EQUIPMENT

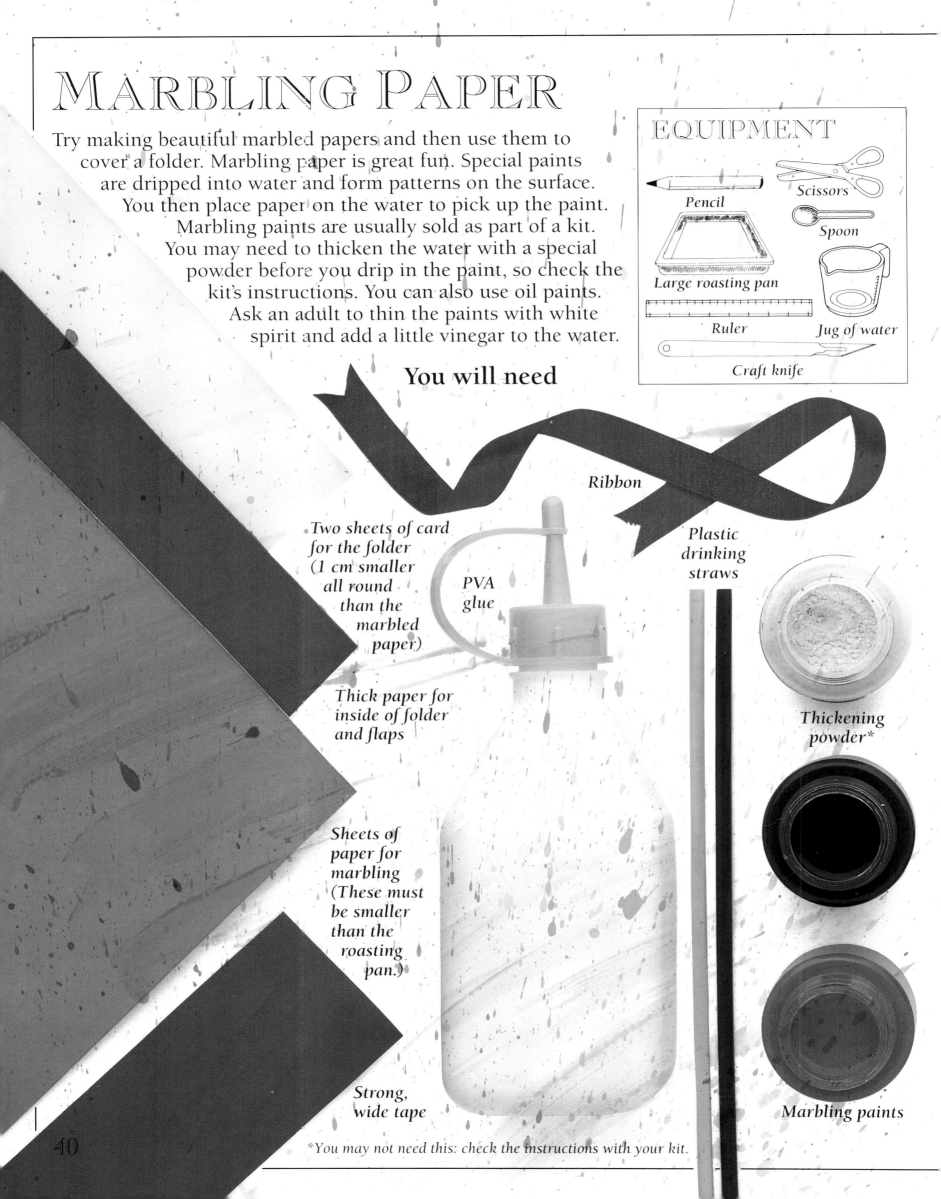

Pencil

Scissors

Spoon

Large roasting pan

Ruler

Jug of water

Craft knife

You will need

Ribbon

Two sheets of card for the folder (1 cm smaller all round than the marbled paper)

PVA glue

Plastic drinking straws

Thickening powder*

Thick paper for inside of folder and flaps

Sheets of paper for marbling (These must be smaller than the roasting pan.)

Strong, wide tape

Marbling paints

40

*You may not need this: check the instructions with your kit.

Marbling the paper

1 Fill a large, old roasting pan with about 2 cm of water**. Use straws to drip a few drops of each paint colour into the water.

2 Gently swirl the paint around with a straw to make a pattern in the water. Burst any bubbles on the surface with the straw.

3 Lay a sheet of paper on the surface of the water, holding it by opposite ends. Gently press down on the paper, as shown.

Making the folder

4 Lift up the paper and put it face up on some newspaper to dry. If you used thickening powder, rinse the wet paper under water.

1 You will need two sheets of marbled paper to make a folder. Glue each sheet to some card to make the two sides of the folder.

2 Ask an adult to cut a small slit in both sides of the folder. Push a length of ribbon through each slit and glue down, as shown.

 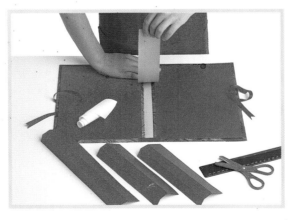 

3 Tape the two outer corners on both sides of the folder. Then glue a sheet of thick paper to the inside of both sides of the folder.

4 Line up the sides of the folder, leaving a 2 cm gap between them. Join them together with two strips of tape. Make three flaps***.

5 Glue the flaps inside the folder on the right-hand side. There should be a tiny space between the flaps so that they fold over easily.

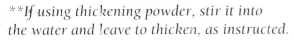

If using thickening powder, stir it into the water and leave to thicken, as instructed.

*** Cut out and fold two flaps for the short edges of the folder and one for the long edge.*

41

Marbled Folders

Choose tape and ribbon for your folder in colours that will go with your marbled papers. You can make different patterns every time you marble a sheet of paper. Experiment by swirling the paint in different directions, or leave it unswirled.

You can also cover notebooks or diaries with your papers, use them as wrapping paper or to make gift bags and gift tags, or simply frame them as pictures.

Strong, wide tape around corners

Ribbon

Strong, wide tape on spine of folder

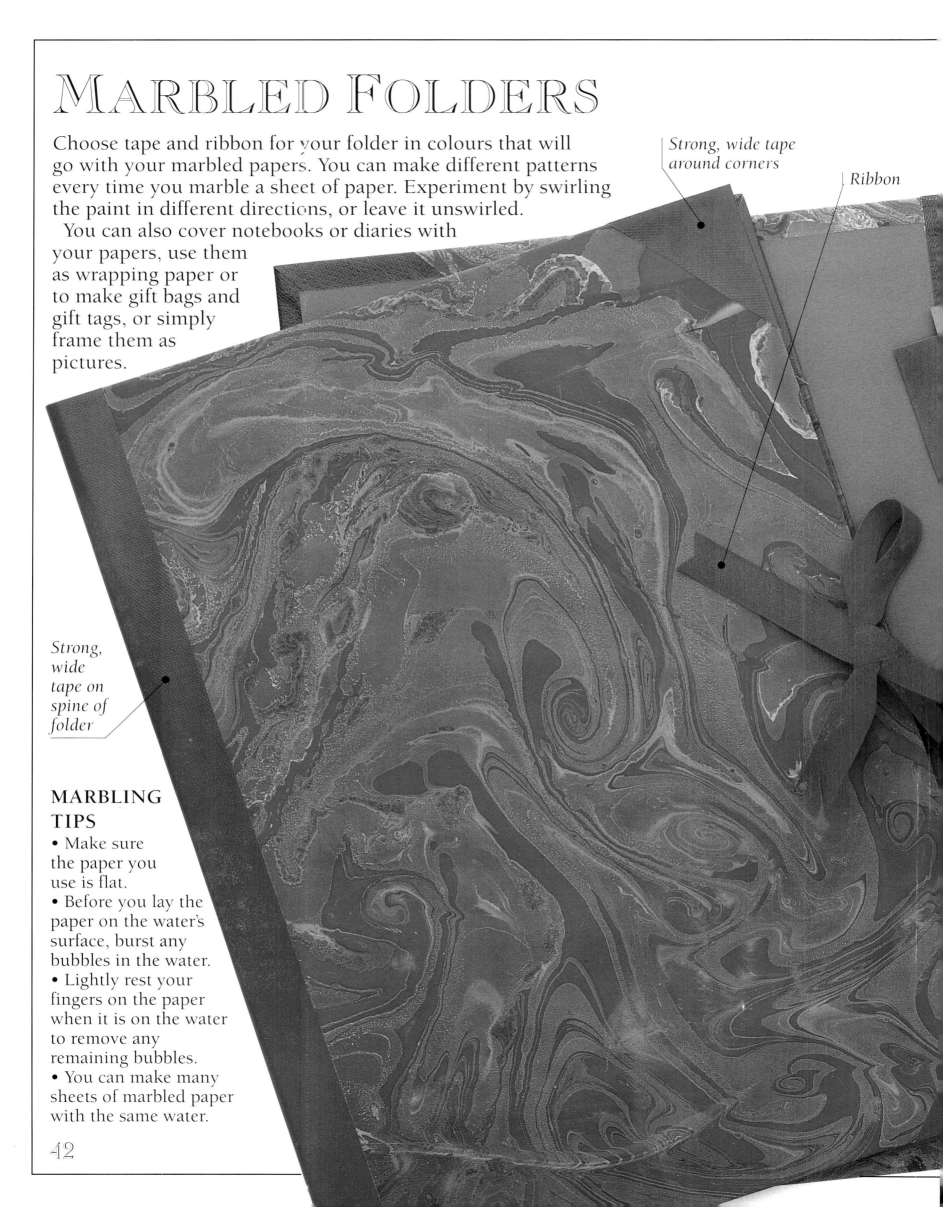

MARBLING TIPS

• Make sure the paper you use is flat.

• Before you lay the paper on the water's surface, burst any bubbles in the water.

• Lightly rest your fingers on the paper when it is on the water to remove any remaining bubbles.

• You can make many sheets of marbled paper with the same water.

The two strips of tape joining
the two sides of the folder
together make a flexible spine.

The three flaps
hold your paper or
pictures in the folder.

*Stick the flaps
a little way in
from the edge
of the folder.*

*Thick paper is used
to make the flaps.*

43

SCRATCH AND SCRAPE

Try scraping marks into thick paint to make a textured painting. You can scratch out all sorts of different patterns. Use flour to thicken ready-mixed, water-based paints. Make sure that the flour is thoroughly mixed into the paint. When painting the picture, work quickly, or the paint will dry before you can scrape it!

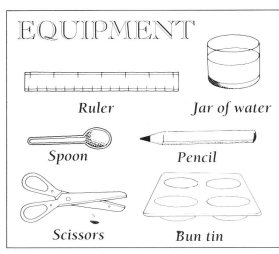

Ruler

Jar of water

Spoon

Pencil

Scissors

Bun tin

You will need

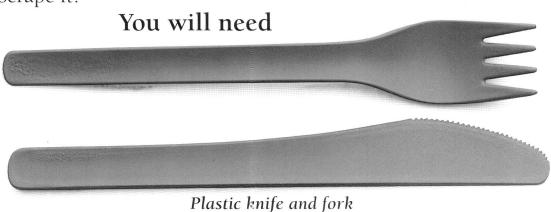

Plastic knife and fork

Paintbrush

Card

Ready-mixed, water-based paints

Flour

PVA glue

Making the picture

1 Cut out a sheet of card for the background. Draw shapes on another sheet of card*. Mix a little flour into each paint colour.

2 Paint the background. Quickly scrape different patterns into the paint with a plastic knife and fork. Do the same with the shapes.

3 When the background and shapes are dry, cut out the shapes, arrange them into a design, and glue them to the background.

*Work out what shapes you will need for your pattern on scrap paper first.

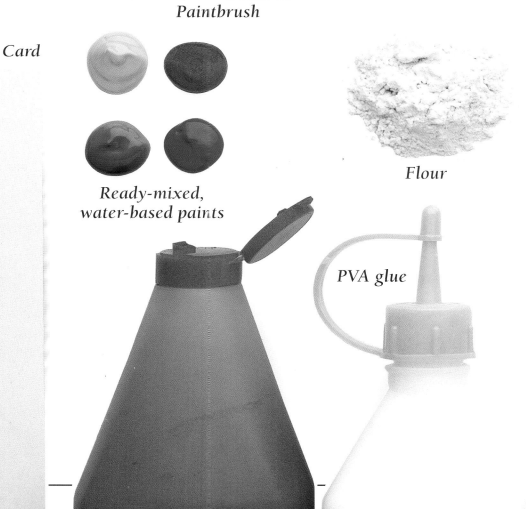

The finished picture

Here, diamonds and strips of card have been arranged to make a colourful pattern.

Diamonds

Strips of card

You can fit your shapes together like a jigsaw.

You can scrape swirls, straight lines, and different shapes into the paint.

This pattern was scraped with the teeth of a fork.

PAPIER-MÂCHÉ FRAME
Turn the page to find out how to mount and frame the picture.

White mount

FUN FRAMES

Frame your favourite paintings and hang them up at home. Below, you can find out how to make picture frames and how to make a "mount". This is some card that surrounds a picture. You don't have to use a mount, but it can help a picture to stand out.

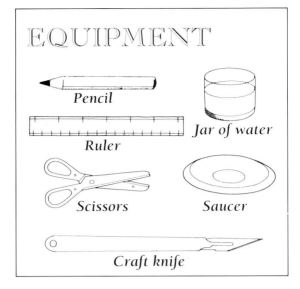

Pencil

Ruler

Jar of water

Scissors

Saucer

Craft knife

You will need

Corrugated card

Thick card

Paintbrush

Papier-mâché

Strong thread

Poster paints

PVA glue

Sticky tape

46

Double card frame

1 Draw a rectangle on card 1 cm bigger all round than the picture you want to frame*. Ask an adult to cut it out to make a frame.

2 Ask an adult to cut out a narrower frame to fit over the first frame, as shown. Glue the frames together. Leave them to dry.

3 Paint the frame. Try printing, splattering, or scratching the paint. Tape the frame to some thick card so that it dries flat.

*If your picture is square or round, draw a square or circle on the card instead.

Mounting the picture

4 Glue your picture to a sheet of card that is the same size as the frame. Then glue the frame to the card and tape thread to the back.

Papier-mâché frame

Ask an adult to cut out a single card frame. You can then thicken the frame with papier-mâché**. Let it dry overnight and then paint it.

Corrugated card frame

Cut out strips of corrugated card and glue them to a single card frame, as shown. When the glue is dry, paint the frame.

**Turn to page 39 for instructions on making papier-mâché.

The frames

Paint your frame and choose a mounting card in a colour to suit the picture you are framing. Look at the frames on this page and on pages 13, 36, 45, and 48 for some ideas.

CORRUGATED CARD FRAME

PAPIER-MÂCHÉ FRAME

DOUBLE CARD FRAME
Turn the page to see a printed double card frame.

Scratched paint (see page 44 for this technique)

Splatter picture (see page 21 for splattering)

The white card mount brings out the white in the splatter pattern.

FRAMING TIPS
• Make sure your picture is in the centre of the frame.
• You can make the frame wide or narrow. Choose a width to suit your picture.
• If you are not using a mount, the frame hole must be slightly smaller than your picture.

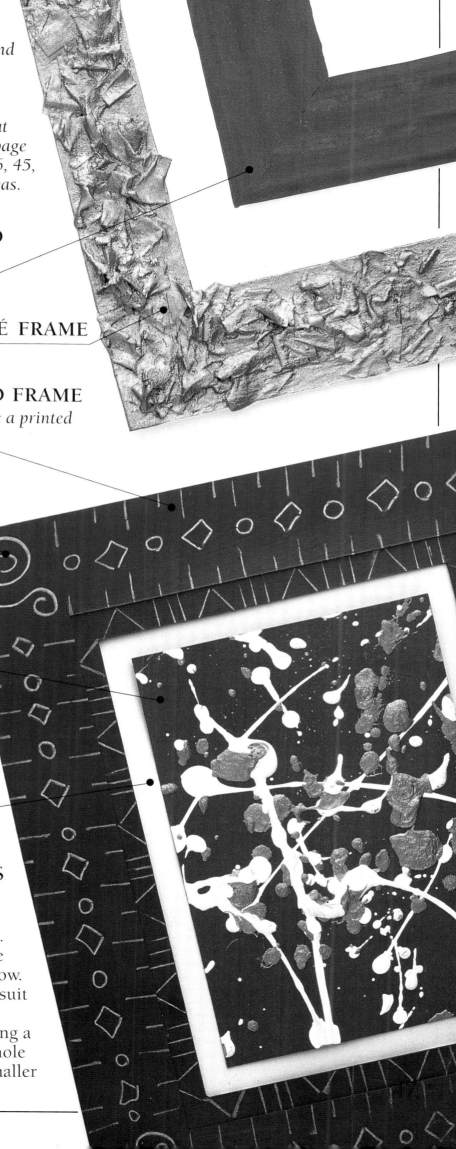

PAINTING TIPS

Practise on scrap paper first to work out your picture, pattern, or design.

If you make a mistake, leave the paint to dry and then paint over it.

When painting on thin card or paper, tape your picture to thick card to stop it curling up as the paint dries.

Change your brush water when it becomes dirty to keep your paint colours clean, and have a rag handy for wiping brushes.

Always put the lids back on your paints to stop them drying out or spilling.

Work near a sink so that you can clean up easily.

Clean brushes thoroughly with soapy water. Ask an adult to help you use white spirit to clean brushes after using oil-based varnish.